OTHER BOOKS B...

ESSENTIAL GEIST:

VOLUME II

Collected Poems & Anecdotes
2016-2019

James Curtis Geist

Walt Whitman is the father of free verse poetry. It uses no formal rhyme scheme, meter, or musical pattern as can be seen in his book <u>Leaves of Grass</u>. Some of the great American free verse poets include Langston Hughes, Carl Sandburg, Ezra Pound, T.S. Eliot, Walt Whitman, Robert Graves, Charles Bukowski, Katherine Foreman, Li-Youn Lee and Nikki Giovanni.

"How can I know what I think till I see what I say?"
-E.M. Forster

"First you're an unknown, then you write a book and
move up to obscurity."
-Martin Meyers

"Bad things don't happen to writers; it's all material."
-Garrison Keillor

"Easy reading is damn hard writing."
-Nathaniel Hawthorne

"If I waited for perfection...I would never write a word.
-Margaret Atwood

"Better to write for yourself and have no public, than to write
for the public and have no self."
-Cyril Connolly

This book comprises
of my favorite poems
from 2016-2019.

TABLE OF CONTENTS

SECTION 1

HORSE SHOE FOR GOOD LUCK (1)

I was 9 years old
when I stayed overnight
at Uncle Dales and
Aunt Sandy's Farm
in Northampton County Pa.

I fed the chickens,
I fed Bucky the Beagle,
I fed the pigs,
I cleaned manure from
the horse stalls and

I fed the horses.
I walked behind the horse
as it was eating and
I feel a gun shot in my
back right side ribs.

I lose my wind,
fly 6-8 feet
into the wet mud
just outside the barn.

I try to catch my breath
and come the realization
how important oxygen
is for quality of life.

I did not feel lucky
this day, even though
I have a bruised
marking of a horse
shoe on my back
from the kicking horse.

SALES PITCH (1)
(circa 1999)

When I work for the man, I complain.
When I am unemployed, I complain
I am not working for the man.
I am conflicted.

I go to an interview for a sales job
in Tarrytown NY, across the
Tappan Zee Bridge.

I have no idea what they sell.
It turns out to be a job selling frozen food
from small refrigerated pick-up trucks
"posing" as restaurant sales vehicles.

We go up to a house wife's,
I mean "homemakers" front door and say,
"I sell to local seafood places and restaurants,
and I have some extra seafood today.
How about some seafood for your fridge?"

As I sit in a drab room
on the dirty tattered carpet,
a woman with long dark hair in a pony tail
walks in the middle of the room
and starts pacing around
preaching in ecstatic tongues

"I love working for this company!
I can make as much money as I want!
When I meet my daily quota, I can go home early!
This job is easy, the product sells itself!"

She is the hype girl of the company
and reminds me of the Ben Affleck
character in the movie Boiler Room.
She was convinced,
she was less convincing to me.

I am sent out with an old timer.
I must give one day of free labor,
"training" to learn the con,
I mean trade.

The "seafood company" sells frozen
     fish,
     shrimp,
     clams,
     scallops
     and lobster

I knew in five minutes
this was not for me,
but I am stuck in training
for another 6 hours and 55 minutes,
and I did not know how to
walk back to the headquarters.
I chose to make the best of it.
It was one of the longest days of my life.

On the way home to the frozen food outlet,
the old white-haired bearded man tried to
convince me how this was a great job.
I tried to convince the old man
how Jesus made a difference in my life.

At least my sales pitch had more conviction.

THE FINICKY BEGGAR (2)
Circa 1995

In Manhattan, I witness
a homeless
couple sitting in front of
a Presbyterian Church
on 5th Avenue, near
Central Park.

Three hours later when
I passed them again,
the male took out a wad
of bills, larger than I
ever held in my hand.

On another occasion,
by Saint John Divine
Church at 112 St. and
Amsterdam Avenue,
was a young man of
color with short hair
and very sweaty.

He walked up to me
and asked for
money. I told him I
would buy him a slice
of pizza if he was

hungry. He said no, he
wanted cash. He was
having a jones for his
drug of choice. He was
the most picky, finicky
and fussy beggar I ever
met.

I said, "I am afraid you
will use the money on
drugs." The beggar
responded he needed a
haircut. I told him I
only give to Salvation
Army and to the Red
Cross.

Sic! (3)

When my grandfather
James C. Short (b. 1923)
was in elementary school,
he was bullied every day
after school.

After his last bullying session,
James Curtis brought his mixed-breed
mutt "Queenie" to the scene of the
crime, pointed his finger at the bullies
and said "Sic!"

His best friend chased them down
and gave them bites
not of the love kind.

In Scottish "sic' equals attack.
In Latin, "sic" translates to
"thus it is written."

Thus it was the last time
the bullies
bullied
James Curtis Short.

THE CALL (4)
1983

Part of my chores at age 17 were doing dishes, collecting the garbage, cleaning up the dog poo and mowing the lawn.

One Saturday summer afternoon, I was mowing the lawn when I thought I heard someone call my name. My parents and sister were away, so I knew it was not one of them.

I had a religious conversion experience in my 9th grade year, and was committed to reading my Bible and going to church. Dad even suggested to me I might consider going into ministry.

I was familiar with in their calling by God was of Abraham and Moses. In both cases, God called their names, and they both responded with "It is I!" In reality, they did not feel worthy or ready to do so, but God promised to guide them in their leadership roles.

I am mowing listening the loud mowing engine noise and I hear, "Jim." I look around at the three properties next to 512 College Drive to see who is calling me. I cannot see anyone. I keep mowing.

Again, I hear a voice calling my name - "Jim!" This time it is louder, and THERE IS STILL NO ONE AROUND.

I start to think, perhaps I am losing my mind, or perhaps, this could be the calling of the Lord. I keep mowing pretending I did not hear anything.

On the third time I hear, "JIM!"

I turn off the mower and I say "Yes Lord, It is I."

AND THEN.....

I hear laughing, and it turns out to me my neighbor, Mr. McCormick, a retired Irish Catholic Gentleman who I can hear wheezing in laughter.

He was sitting in his bedroom, but I could not see him because that corner of his house was covered in shade. In his Irish brogue, he tells me, "Oh Jimmy, Jimmy. You just made my day!"

I ended up going into ministry for five years, and ended up following my bliss by becoming a teacher in New York City. There are many similarities with teaching and ministry. My psychological makeup test tells me my temperament is best for being a counselor, teacher or minister.

On that fine Summer day in 1983, I was ready and willing to serve.

ELEMENTARY SCHOOL PORN (5)
1971

The Supreme Court does not give a
specific definition for pornography – you
know what pornography is when you see it.

In the Library as I peruse Sports Illustrated,
and some National Geographic Magazines,
there is an article with pictures about a group
of people recently discovered called the Tasaday
in the Philippines, who have never met modern
people. They are called Stone Age People.
In the pics, the woman are not wearing tops.

> I cannot stop staring at the breasts of the
> Tasaday women. My second grade
> teacher sneaks up to my table and says,
> "I knew it, put that down."

My excitement turns to shame.
How can something "bad"
for viewing enjoyment be
allowed in the elementary
school library?

> As Jimmy Kimmel and Adam
> Carola of The Man Show
> (1999-2004) answer:
> "Why do men love boobs?"
> is the same as asking
> "Why do men breathe?"

HAPPINESS WHEN... (6)

I will be happy when...

I graduate from elementary school;
I get a puppy;
I move from junior high school;
I get my driver's license;
I get a job and some spending money;
I get a girlfriend;
I graduate from high school;
I get my own car;
I graduate from college;
I get my own apartment;
I get my career;
I get married;
I buy my first home;
I get a promotion at work;
I have children;
I write a book;
I get a divorce to be free;
I find a hot girlfriend;
I buy a bigger house;
I buy a nicer car;
I retire;

OR - I could choose to be content right now.

I choose to live a life of joy and contentment daily.

Attitude is everything...and free.

MY KID POLTER GEIST (7)

I wanted to name
my first child
Polter.
The wife said no.

My wife's
new name
is ex.

If I named my child,
I would name him/her
Doctor,
Professor,
President,
Principal,
or
General.

I could save the child
much time
from
college,
grad school,
service and
money.

No wasted time.
No debt.

GRINGO HALLOWEEN (7)
circa 1994 – Corona Queens

Elmhurst Queens is the most ethnically diverse area of the United States. I work for New Life Fellowship Church located at the Elks Lodge in Elmhurst.

The Church Offices are in Corona Queens, home the Lemon Ice King, and ½ a mile away from Shea Stadium, home of the Mets. Just around the corner is a donut shop the singer Madonna use to work before becoming a star. It is the Corona Paul Simon sings about in "Me and Julio down in the school yard."

Below our offices is an awesome restaurant that makes the best chicken, rice and beans around. It is Halloween Day, and I stop by to say hello, and the kiddies are dressed up and getting candy from the restaurant hostess.

The restaurant owners are Cuban, and used to have a restaurant in China making Spanish food, and they moved into Queens. The owners speak Spanish, Chinese and English.

I ask the hostess for some Halloween candy. She says, "Mister, you need to have a costume on." In front of the owners, the bus boy, the servers and the hostess I say, "I am dressed up for Halloween. I am dressed as a Gringo!"

They all laugh; but I laugh hardest with candy in hand.

ERIN GO BRAUGH - "Ireland Forever!"

Druids Bar (50th St. & 11th Ave NYC),
Hell's Kitchen – St. Patrick's Day – 2,000.

It is my second year teaching at Park West High
School, and I am invited to the famous Saint
Patrick's Day meal of corn beef, cabbage,
potatoes and carrots with my teaching mates.

I have never partaken before, and the corn beef
high in fat, washed down with pints of Guinness
and the cabbage that breaks down
into methane, carbon dioxide and hydrogen
begin to fill my belly just before bedtime.

I lay on the floor in the fetal position,
in my 3rd floor apartment in Queens,
feeling as though I am giving birth, I
make groaning noises and keep
saying, "Never again!"

The experience is so traumatizing, it is
five years before I touch cabbage again.
When I do, I take a beano pill, and eat one
small helping to avoid my innards
contraction pains caused by gas.

Erin go braugh? More like
Erin needs to go to the Emergency Room.

SECTION 2

VAGAL REFLEX (1)
(circa 1994)

I enter entered the Veteran's of Foreign Wars
Reception Hall on Sumner Avenue
in Allentown Pennsylvania
for the 1994 annual Geist Christmas Party
and hang my jacket.

Cousin Cindy and her three year old son Brandon
with bright red hair,
walk through the entry doors.
He would be my second cousin.

I bend over to introduce myself to Brandon
who has never met me,
and who has been taking karate classes
and learning about "stranger danger."
Faster than I can blink my eyes,
he socks me in the scrotum
with his karate fist punch.

I feel pain in my groin area
and my stomach immediately feels nauseated.
The blow to my scrotum sack,
full of tender-spongy-fleshy-testes
sends a message through the nerves
to my brain back down to my stomach.
This kid's teacher must be Bruce Lee.

24

It is worse than an ice cream head ache,
because the pain from
the kick,
punch,
or baseball
into the nuts lasts longer.

The pain is the combination
of getting the wind knocked out
from a football tackle,
or a kick ball kicked
straight to the stomach,
AND of a dentist
sticking his sharp hooked metal probe
into the nerve of a bad tooth.

During turkey season 12 years later,
I want to slather a dap of Icy Hot
in Brandon's underwear
while he takes a shower but I don't;
he was just a kid at the time of
the Karate Kid Uppercut to "the boys."

I am glad I don't give child birth.

ELKS LODGE BEAUTY CONTEST (1)
(circa 2015)

The pork chops, sour kraut and

mashed potato dinner is filling.

The rock band is fairly good.

The square bar is full of round people

as I sit at a small high table

against the back wall with Tiffany.

She is a blond with blue eyes and shapely.

A drunk woman passes us

on the way to the bathroom,

she points at Tiffany and says,

"You are beautiful."

The drunk points at me,

loses her smile and says,

"You are okay looking."

The drunk says what

the sober person thinks.

HARLEM MOCKING BIRD ATTACK (2)

On June 16th, 2017, I attend the NABIG or the North
American Basic Income Guarantee Congress at the
Silberman School of Social Work at Hunter College on
116th St. and 3rd Avenue in the Harlem section of
Manhattan.

During the lunch break, I head out to the outside courtyard
on the second floor with over a dozen tables. No one is in
the courtyard. I go to the farthest table to enjoy my brown
bagged lunch and coffee.

Fifteen feet from me on a black metal railing, a bird lights
on the railing and starts squawking at me. It seems very
upset and I tell it to bugger off. The bird looks like a
miniature flying road runner to me, I have never seen a
bird like this. This bird is jumping up and down in a fit.

The bird flies at my face. I throw my silver coffee
container into my lunch carrier, and with my other hand,
hold my satchel bag over my head as I start running
towards the building doors fifty feet away.

A security agent witnesses the action, and laughs and
walkie-talkies his boss and several other agents. Of course,
when they walked out on the courtyard, the bird is not to
be seen. Ten minutes later I walked outside the door for 10
seconds, and the bird from 50 yards away aims for my
head again.

I recollect videos of mocking birds dive bombing pedestrians walking past trees with their nests above on You Tube.

In the book <u>To Kill a Mocking Bird,</u> attorney father Atticus Finch says, "…it is a sin to kill a mocking bird." Trust you me, if I had a tennis racket with me, I would smacked this angry dive bombing mocking bird into eternity.

I would have placed the bird under a park bench for a stray cat to enjoy for dinner.

GARDEN HOSE FAUCET (2)

Garden
hose
faucet -

lefty
loosey,
righty
tighty,

if
not;

the
opposite.

YES SIR MADAME TEACHER (3)
(circa 1975)

Mrs. Becker was my music teacher
at Union Terrace Elementary
in fourth grade aged 9.
The boys use to argue
"If you had to marry the
Music, Art or Gym teacher,
which one?" I always chose
Ms. Gatos the art teacher,
others Ms. Carol.

I had just seen a military movie
over the weekend and the soldiers
kept saying "Yes Sir!" or "No Sir!"

In music class I am in the back row
Fooling around and not paying attention
And we are singing
John Jacob Jingle Heimer Schmidt
or Swing Low Sweet Chariots or
Jimmy Crack Corn when -

Mrs. Becker calls my name.
Thinking I am showing respect,
I say "Yes Sir!"
She gets up from her synthesizer seat,
briskly walks over to the back row
and picks me up by the back curlies
of my reddish hair.

"WHAT DID YOU SAY?"
"Yes Sir?"
"I AM TO BE CALLED MAM!"

I learned something that day.

MY LAST CHURCH PLAY (4)
1985

I was fortunate to be part of the Hamilton Park Church on
Ott Street and Flexer Avenue in Allentown. It was
composed of many loving and supportive people who took
interest in me, and gave me love, prayer and
encouragement.

Mrs. Van Skyke was my Sunday School Teacher, and after
high school, I went to Nyack College, affiliated with the
Christian and Missionary Alliance with Karen Van Skyke.

Every Christmas, Mrs. Van Skyke was in charge of the
Christmas play. Little did I know, she had put me in a
role in the Church Play in our little church of 75 people.

I was looking forward to good food, sleeping and hanging
out with friends. I needed a break from the books. I was
mentally exhausted from classes, taking notes, reading and
writing papers. The last thing I wanted to do was to do any
reading or memorization over the break.

I walk into the house, and Mom hands me the script for the
upcoming play.

I say, "What is this?"
Mom responds, "Mrs. Van Skyke has you in the Christmas
play."
I respond with "WHAT????"

I accept my fate and try to make the best of it. I also make it clear to Mrs. Van Skyke this will be my last church play.

I play a father in the play, and my sister Jody plays the role of my daughter in the play. I memorize my lines, go to the rehearsals and we finally have our big show, and I make it through the whole play remembering all my lines.

The last line of the play is when I compliment my daughter by saying, "I am so proud of you my little Mahalia!"

I am so happy the play is coming to a close, but I cannot fully remember the last line.

I say, "I am so proud of you......"
Darn, what is my daughter's name?

I try again, "I am so proud of you...."
Why can't I remember my daughter's name?

I try one more time.

"I am so proud of you......
And then I say - "What is you name again?"

The church audience breaks out into a roar, and I am sure it is a memory many remember for years. Many said, that moment made the play.

For me, it is a memory I will never forget.

DO YOU MODEL? (5)
1983

It is the Springtime of my Junior year.
I read the paper and look at some of
the local models used on the Hess
Department Store adds page.

I am aged 17 and swing by
Carvel Ice Cream for a cone.
The young lady with blond hair
looks like one of the models in
the Morning Call advertisement.

I ask the female ice cream slinger
if she did any modeling for Hess.
She grimaces and says, "That is the
worst pick up line I have ever heard."

I go home, rip out the advertisement
from the paper and drive back to Carvel.
I walk up to the blondie
and hand her the paper.

As I walk away, I overhear her
fellow Carvel Ice Cream worker say,
"That does look like you!"

It was not a pick up line,
yet I would not have objected to
picking up the slinger for a date.

I am called in for a substitute teaching assignment for the school's German teacher who is named Ms. Early.

I report to the school office and Mary Ann the executive school secretary calls my name. She pulls out a small orange sheet of paper, writes out 1 through 8 and begins putting room numbers next to each number plus my lunch period.

There are several types of schedules the school follows when not on a "regular schedule." There is a delayed opening, early dismissal, double first, double second, double third and pep rally.

The secretary says, "You are the German teacher today - you are on the Early schedule."

I say, "We are on an early schedule today?"

Mary Ann says, "Who said we are on an early schedule? Where did you get that idea?"

I say, "I could have sworn you said we are on the early schedule."

She asks the other secretary, "Are we on the early schedule today?" The other secretary says, "No, it is a regular schedule today."

The subbing secretary does not suffer fools well, so I choose to keep quiet. I can choose to be right and keep my peace.

She double checks my schedule and says, "Okay, here is the schedule for the German teacher, Ms. Early."

I say, "That is why I thought you said we were on an "Early Schedule" today. When you first called me, you told me, you are on the Early schedule."

She shakes her head and smiles.

See, I was on the Early schedule (the teacher), not the "early schedule" when classes are shortened and the kids are dismissed at 12:19.

Who is on first base?

In June the wife goes in for a physical with our doctor. The doctor gives us a prescription for a mammogram. We go to the hospital to set up a date. They give us a phone number to call. I call.

Hello. I need a date for my wife to get a mammogram.

Uh-huh. Blue Cross-Blue Shield is what we have. Yes, next Thursday will work.

Is she pregnant? I don't think so. If she is, it is not mine, I had a vasectomy. If she is pregnant, we got a problem!

Helen, are you pregnant?

She tells me no, because if it was yes, my next call would be to my attorney.

The ladies at the front desk
have a "shocked and awe"
look on their mugs.

FORTY-EIGHT (8)

Since 1999, there have
been ten school shootings in which five or
more persons were killed.

Since 1982-2012 of
the 143 weapons, more than half of the
mass shooters possessed had
high-capacity magazines, assault weapons or both.

Of the 143 guns
used in mass shootings, **48** would have been
banned by the Assault
Weapons ban of 2013 introduced one month after
the December 14, 2012
Sandy Hook School shooting killing 20 children &
6 teachers in Newtown.

This was the day our
Senate chose N.R.A. campaign bribes with the 40-
60 vote denying the
public who supported Assault Weapon Ban(S.150)
despite 90% supporting it.

SECTION 3

THE KING AND DOG (1)

I am the king when I get a tax refund,
I am the dog when I owe.

I am the king when I win an award,
I am the dog when I get a poor performance review.

I am the king when my dental check-up shows no cavities,
I am the dog when I need a root canal.

I am the king when I find money on the street,
I am the dog when I lose my wallet.

I am the king when the house is running well,
I am the dog when the hot water heater breaks down.

I am the king when I marry or get in a new relationship.
I am the dog when I divorce or there is the heartbreak.

I am the king when my sports teams win a championship,
I am a dog when they lose the championship.

I am the king when I am healthy,
I am the dog when I end up in the emergency room.

I am the king when my stock portfolio is doing well,
I am the dog when the market crashes.

I am the king when I have freedom,
I am the dog when I have to go to court as a defendant.

Being king is great, being the dog is not the worst,
for any day above ground is a good day.

PARTIAL DENTURES (1)

I have a renter named Barry.
His estranged wife uses him
as an ATM machine for child support and alimony.
He works at West Point as a general laborer
and rarely pays his full rent.

He falls in love with
a dancer in Newark named Candy,
and he buys her cigarettes and drinks.
He does not buy her $5 beers,
she "only drinks the $10 shots."

While Barry paid money to sleep with her twice,
he claims she is not a hooker.
He also believes Candy is his girlfriend,
even though he has met her boyfriend.

When Barry was 9 he fell riding his bicycle
and smashed his face into the curb
breaking four of his front teeth.
He keeps the partials in a glass of water
on shelf above the toilet.
When the partials are in the glass,
I know Barry is home.

He gets a 30,000 inheritance from his
parent's estate, and buys a blue Ford
Mustang for $10,000, he even loans
money to Candy to bail her out of the tank.
I never see the back rent from his 30K.

I like Barry, a PTSD survivor
from his Army time in the Iraq.
Some drunks made fun of Barry's wrinkled
army outfit he wears to the bar Veterans
Day for free drinks.

Barry moved out and I miss is guitar
playing.   I use his former denture glass to
drink whiskey and water or a rum and coke
sans the dental partials and salute him.

DEATH BY PAINTING (2)

Climb the 32 foot ladder
to paint soffits
below the gutters.

Scrape, scrape, scrape.
Spackle, spackle, spackle.
Sand, sand, sand.
Brush, brush, brush the primer.
Move ladder and repeat.

Working with an
entertaining crew of saltys
in A.A., N.A.
or active in their addictions.

Hornets nest,
fly down the ladder,
climb back up
with the wasp spray.
No stings today.

Once between the eyes,
my head swelled like a melon
and my eyes turned Asian.

Climb ladder.
Scrape.
Spackle.
Sanding.
Priming.
Move ladder.

Change the radio station.
Wash out the brush
using the garden hose
and wire brush.

First coat of finish.
Move ladder.

Coffee break.

Second coat of finish.
Move to the
other side of house
and repeat.

LUNCH;
actually
watch
paint
dry
on
walls.

Sun in eyes,
sweat in eyes,
paint droplets
in eyes and ears.

Left knee
sometimes aches,
some get tennis elbow,
is there a painter's
elbow syndrome?

43

I scratch an itch
on my face accidently
giving myself
a make out bandit
paint mustache.

Feeling tired from
physical labor,
heat and humidity,
I drink another coffee
and turn up the radio
and find the strength
to make it to 4:30pm.

Wax on, wax off.
paint up, paint down.
According to the
Karate Kid movie
And Mr. Miyagi,
I should have
been a martial arts
expert a decade ago.
It must feel powerful
to know you can kill a
man with your hands.

Paint chips in
my socks, shoes
underwear and hair.
At least a root canal only
lasts for an hour.

A GIFT FROM THE FOREST GOD (3)

I love the woods.
I enjoy hiking.
I hate litter.

Helen and I walk
to the parking lot
of Waywayanda
State Park in N.J.
after our Eagle
Rock Trail hike –

someone has dumped
garbage in the woods
next to the lot.

Why would someone
enjoy nature,
only too lazy,
too uncivil,
to unconscious
to carry the
trash home?

Take photographs,
leave only footprints.

A homemade sign
off a Whitehall Pennsylvania
country road says,

"Litter Bugs
are trash!"

I grab a garbage
bag from the auto,
pick up the garbage,
and among the trash
I find a $1 bill.

It a gift from
the forest God
saying, "Go buy
a drink, but please
place the plastic
bottle in recycling."

THANKS!

I listen to
"Rocky Mountain High"
by John Denver on
the drive home.

DRILL SERGEANT (3)

(circa 1973)

Jimmy the Barber is

one of the shining jewels

of West Milford NJ,

a very funny man and

musician in The Rock-a-holics.

Jimmy was drafted for the Vietnam War,

and his basic training sergeant,

was a skinny black man

with the protruding

chicken barrel chest –

turning civilians into soldiers

is a serious and daunting task.

The recruits were a mixture of

white and black men,

many of whom were out of shape.

Jimmy will never forget his first

day of basic training when

the Drill Sergeant screamed,

"I only hate two kinds of people!

fat people

and

white people!"

YES SIR!

THE WIND CRIES MARY (4)
1994

As a graduate student, I lived at the home of Mary Grace.
I lived in her for four years, from her 80th to 84th year. She
was progressive and use to be one of the "flappers."

She also worked as an assistant Editor at Fortune Magazine
for 40 years. She was smart, witty and kept up with
modern culture by reading the NY Times every Wednesday
and Sunday. On Mondays she went into NYC to make
recordings for the blind.

She passed in 1994, and I wept like a baby, for she had
become a grandmotherly figure in my life.

Her son Danny, worked for the New Yorker Magazine said
as a thank you, my wife Tersea Joy and I could have any
piece of furniture in the house. We chose the Chippendale
wooden secretary. The day I stopped by to clean it out, I
put the radio on, and the song, "The Wind Cries Mary,"
was playing on the radio. It brought tears to my eyes.

A few weeks later after the Memorial Service in Grand
View, just down the road from Nyack, on our way back to
NYC, as Teresa Joy and I were crossing the Tappan Zee
Bridge, I put on the radio, and the song, "The Wind Cries
Mary" was on the radio. It caused me to cry a second time.
I could not believe a loss could hurt so much.

I still get chills thinking how the Jimi Hendrix song came
up on two occasions after the passing of Mary Grace.

BROKEN DOWN FREIGHTLINER (5)

My Grandfather, Father, Uncles
and many family friends worked
the assembly line at Mack Trucks.

Whenever Dad met a truck driver,
he would ask him, "What truck
do you drive?"

If it was a non-Mack truck, Dad would
Say, "Oh, aren't those the ones I
usually see broken down on the side of
roads?"

 The trucker laughed knowing Dad
was a Mack worker.

The Mack workers took pride in
    their work,
        their quality product
            and loved the saying:

"Built Like A Mack Truck!"

50

FUTURE TEACHERS OF AMERICA (6)

At the beginning of the school year, I asked all my students what they wanted to do for a living. I had three smart young ladies who all said "Teachers!"

At the end of the semester, I asked the students again, what they wanted to do for a living when they finished college, and everyone gave the same answers, until I got to the three smart young ladies.

This time they answered "Nurses!" I asked them why they changed their minds from teaching to nursing they said, "After sitting in your class, we realized how disrespectful many of your students are.

Did I mention these young ladies were smart?

THE PRICE OF TRUTH TELLING (7)

The Old Testament Prophets

Jesus

John Brown

President Abraham Lincoln

Pontiac

The Molly Maguires

Governor Huey Long

Gandhi

Malcolm X

John F. Kennedy

Martin Luther King

Bobby Kennedy

Harvey Milk

Karen Silkwood

Bishop Oscar Romero

Those who challenge the power structures
often expire early.

10th GRADE SPANISH CLASS (8)
Circa 1981

Ms. Bennett was our teacher
at William Allen High School
in Allentown Pennsylvania.

I sat next to Alicia, Joy and Andrea.
They were hot-ties.

As a new evangelical convert, I brought my Bible to class
and the three hot-ties made much fun of me.

Is that a Bible? Who brings a Bible to school?
YOU, are a loser!
You must blow dry your hair; it look like
a dried out hay bail!

Andrea died of an drug overdose at age 20.
Joy died of cancer at age 30.

Alicia I re-connected with on Facebook 34 years later in
2015. Alicia was a recovering heroin addict, and I
was grateful she was in program.

I was sad to hear of the passing of Andrea and Joy.   If we
they were still alive, I am sure we all had gone to a bar
in the 2,000s and would have gotten along and even
laughed as we shared stories about Allen High and
about life.
No hay mal que cien anos dure.
There is nothing bad that lasts 100 years.
...not even 10-20 years sometimes.

53

SECTION 4

NEMESIS [2011] (1)

I dated a Filipina for two years.
Her name was Teresa, a newspaper reporter
for a local paper in northern New Jersey.
We decided to cohabite before getting married,
to see if her 10 year old daughter
was going to accept me as a step-Dad.

I painted Natalia's room pink,
her favorite color and
put up shelving to make room
for all her toys and stuffed animals.
I took her out for pizza and to the movies.
For her birthday I gave her a card full of money.
I use to take her to the kiddie park in Warwick NY.

I vacuumed the house weekly.
One day I used the sweeper in Natalia's room and
the card I bought her fell off the book shelf.
My name on the card was crossed out,
And underneath was written "NEMESIS."

I opened up my heart and home to this young child,
and I think she was afraid I was stealing
some of her mother's love for her.
It became clear it was not going to work out,
and they moved back in with Teresa's mother.

Maybe the child will one day find out
she does not live with her father,
because he use to beat up her mother.
Perhaps one day she will realize
her half-sister is the result of an adulterous affair.

While I felt betrayed by the child,
I am still impressed a 10 year old
knew what nemesis meant.

Good Bye Dream (2)
(circa 2010)

I taught in NYC for 13 years.
for seven years,
I taught at Park West
and a motherly woman
names Natalie Gutter
(pronounced Goo-ter)
was in my
Social Studies department.

My first year teaching
was in 1999.
Ms. Gutter was always
kind,
encouraging,
and laughed easily.

When not giving me
suggestions on how to
teach a unit,
or talking about
the goofy politics of George W. Bush,
or the United Federation of Teachers,
she talked about her daughter
and grand kids.

I loved when she
rolled her eyes
when the Principal
or Assistant Principal

gave us a silly idea or
directive to carry out.

She retired after
Mayor Bloomberg closed
Park West High at
525 50th Street (11th Ave)
And I was transferred up uptown
to George Washington Campus
in Washington Heights
where
Alan Greenspan,
Henry Kissenger,
Harry Belefonte,
Manny Ramirez
and Lou Alcinder aka
Kareem Abdul Jabar
attended.

I had a dream in
2012 (approximately)
and it was of Ms. Gutter
and I sitting at a café table,
held a discussion and
she said good bye to me
and I said good bye to her.

Funny thing
a person
popping up in a dream
that I had not thought
of in years.

Later in the day,
I received an e-mail
from a former co-worker
telling me Natalie had
Passed the night before.

In my spirit,
I already
intuited
her
passing.

Courtesan Story #2 (3)
(circa 1994)

I am coming home from a Bible Study
I use to lead in Jackson Heights in Queens
at Charles and Mirna's home. It is near
La Guardia Airport, and a large plane
taking off flies over every 5 minutes
shaking the apartment as we "fellowship."

At the street corner across from a
Shop Rite is a woman on the corner
looking in and out of her purse,
looking up to the sky,
walking around and looking on
the ground for something.

I roll the window down in the 1979
sky blue Oldsmobile my Nana and
Grandpa Short gave to me as a gift.

Everything Okay?
"No. I had some money, and now I can't find it.
I had my five dollars in Shop Rite, but now I
can't find it! Can you help me find it?"

I pull the car over and we walk over to
the food store with her.

What do you do for a living?
"I am a hair dresser."

I can tell by her dog breath and unkempt look

and hooker outfit, she is a lady of the evening.
As we get closer to the store, I think, she is
just hoping I give her $5 as a gift. We walk into
the store and I say, *Let's retrace your steps.*

We walk over to the meat isle,
and she says, "I was standing over here
checking out the prices, then I walked
out of the store.

I stand and begin looking up and down
the white and green Mauorette linoleum
flooring in the flickering mood lighting
of store florescent light bulbs.

I pray, "God please help me. How can I really
help this woman?" I feel the urge to get down on
my knees where the meat aisle cooler metaling
meets the floor, I see a small corner of paper
dark green, light green and some black ink.

I grab it with my finger nails, and I pull out
what turns out to be a $5 dollar bill.

"Does this look familiar Ma'am?"

Like the poor old woman in the gospels who
lost a coin celebrating when she finds it again,
the hooker smiles nodding her head with
the "I told you so" look.

DEER, TURKEY, COYOTE, BEAR? (4)
Tall Pines Camp -1987

I am at the Tall Pines Camp in May of 1987 in Central Pennsylvania. It is time for the Spring Gobbler hunting in the morning and trout fishing in the afternoon. There is a decent crew of guys in the four different rooms at the camp. It is always a great time. We even have a trophy for the biggest fish and biggest gobbler.

With Spring Gobbler, you get up at 4:30am, and get to a spot where you hope to call in a Gobbler with a hen call. Hunters dress in camouflage, and it is important you do not move when calling in a bird.

The evening before, I read an Outdoor Life Issue, and it has a story of a turkey hunter who thought he was calling in turkey, but was surprised when jumped by a bobcat. He was not hurt, just a few scratches.

The sun is coming up, I give a few calls, and I hear something sneaking up behind me. I am on the ground sitting against a tree stump, and my heart starts beating. *Wow, this could be a turkey. Or - it could be a deer, or a coyote, or a bear, or a bobcat.*

No sooner does the thought cross my mind when something lands on my shoulder and I jump up and scream like a little girl. I thought I was going to have a heart attack! The shuffling in the leaves and grass I heard, turns out to be s gray squirrel that mistook me for part of the tree stump. *Stupid squirrels!*

QUEENS LAUNDROMAT ROBBERY (4)
circa Fall of 2,000

I lived in Queens on the border of Long Island City and Astoria, there was laundromat down the street on the corner. The lady who worked there spoke Spanish and the ladies loved the gossip.

I laundered my clothing weekly. My modus operandi was to take the clothes to the laundromat and throw them in the washer. I walked back to my apartment.

Twenty minutes later, walked back to the laundromat, took the clothes out of the washer and threw them in the dryer. I walked back to the apartment.

Thirty-five minutes later, I went back to pick up my clothing. I folded the clothes, put them in the basket, and carried the basket back to my apartment at 34-09 41st Street, up to the third floor 3C apartment.

I bought four new dress shirts from Old Navy to use as a substitute teacher, and threw the clothing in the laundry basket to be cleaned. I followed my usual laundromat routine until finished.

I began putting my clothing away at home and just felt something was wrong. I stood there looking at the empty basket on my bed, when it hit me; where are my new shirts? *I was robbed!*

I went back to Old Navy, re-bought four more shirts, and always kept an eye out in my neighborhood for those stolen shirts. I never saw my spiffy stolen shirts again.

I began bringing a book to the laundromat and never left the scene of the crime again, until the final drying and folding of my clothing.

THE WIPE OUT (5)
1979

I had a morning paper route at age 13. It was Route 279, and I delivered to 75 homes. The papers were biggest on Thursday and on Sundays. I would tie a metal cart on my bike to haul the papers to my route on those days.

The best part of newspaper delivery was riding the bike home. I would go home, hang up my three paper bags, and put the bicycle and cart in its assigned spots in the back yard.

One day I was flying down College Drive to our home, and I made my left-handed turn to go up the driveway, my bike went off balance from the weight, speed and awkward angle of the cart on the back of the bicycle....and I wiped out on the driveway of my home.

I lay there with the bike on top of me, and laying there, with my skinned left elbow and knee, I witnessed the window curtains of my sister's room opening slowly. My sister stood there, looked at my plight, and a slight smile came upon her face. It was if the spirit of Damien from the movie the Omen had possessed her.

The window curtains closed as slowly as they originally opened.

NAPPER OR CORPSE? (6)
Saturday June 2nd, 2018

From the Wildwood Crest third floor hotel room balcony is a veranda on the second floor above a beach room in front of our room. It has a canvas roof and has tables and chairs on it for people to take in the beach, ocean, pool and hot tub patrons.

It is raining and cool in the early afternoon, and there is a gentleman in his late 60's, who looks like a golfer, in shorts, a hooded sweatshirt, baseball hat, and towels over his legs, laying there. **Is he napping or deceased?**   I do not see his chest moving up or down. His mouth is open and I do not witness any breathing. On the table next to him are binoculars and a can of Sunkist soda. He looks 85% peaceful.

It is bad enough Anthony Bourdain's, chef, author and television show host of CNN's weekly show, "Parts Unknown," committed suicide the day before. Bourdain is a native son of the New Jersey shore, and a recovering heroin and cocaine addict since his college days, and is known to suffer from depression.

After dinner the lawn chair golfer looking man is gone. Either he woke up (God help him), or the life guard found him and the coroner took the body away (RIP).

Either way, I did not want to waste my weekend being interviewed by police and filling out reports. I was too busy doing nothing.

SUNDAY RITUAL (7)

I tune into Public Radio Sunday afternoons of
Big Band, Jazz and Blues music; it connects
me to an image of my being in the home of my
Grandpa and Nana Short's or Nana and Pappy
Geist's during this time period on a lazy
Saturday or Sunday afternoon while I re-fill the
pill boxes for wife and myself in 2018.

I pull out the eight bottles of vitamins and
prescriptions to make sure my body is not
deficient of minerals and medicine to make the
body function and to help it fight diseases.

In the last three years, I have had health
coverage for only 6 months. Due to the cost of
medication, many of my pills I must cut in
half to make them last.

ESPOUSA

M: Multi-vitamin, Vitamin C, Iron pill,
   Vitamin D pill.
T: Repeat
W: Do Again
Th: Refill
F: Repeat
Sa: Do Again
Su: Refill

MOI

M: Multi-vitamin, Vit. C, Vit. D, Viibryd,
    Blood Pressure pills.
T: Repeat
W: Do Again
Th: Refill
F: Repeat
Sa: Do Again
Su: Refill

It is an act of self-love in wanting to enjoy a life of reasonable health and contentment while enjoying a ritual connecting me to my grandparent and parent's generation.

INTIMACY BIGFOOT-BLOCKED (8)
circa 2006

As a child I learn there are not such things as the
Frankenstein monster, werewolves, or vampires, but
then learn about ghosts, demons, UFO's and aliens.
Great! By great I mean "not really great."

In 1976, some adult takes me to see the movie
"Legend of Bigfoot," which includes a 53 second clip
of a home movie camera shot of a bigfoot given the
name "Patty." I am horrified yet intrigued by this
home movie clip the rest of my living days.

The infamous clip was filmed on October 20th, 1967 by
Roger Patterson and Robert Gimlin while horseback
riding in Bluff Creek California by a tributary of the
Klamath River. Patterson on his deathbed in 1972 said
the creature was real; Gimlin, alive in 2018, swears
the video was not set up or fake.

Scanning through t.v. channels circa 2006, I come
across a documentary on Bigfoot I have never seen. I
have seen it all on Bigfoot, Hairy Man, Sasquatch, or
the Wild Man - I believe. What Peanuts character
Linus is to the Great Pumpkin, I am to Bigfoot.

I sit back with my beer and pop-corn sitting back on
the Lazy Boy. Mind you, this is before the weekly
Animal Planet television series, "Finding Bigfoot,"
and I have not seen any shows on Bigfoot in years. I
am the kid in the candy store as this documentary
starts.

68

Mind you, this is before the Animal Planet program "Finding Bigfoot" that runs from 2011 through 2018. Any new video of the beast or credible testimony has my fullest attention, especially before 2011, IS MUST WATCH VIEWING for me.

The 2006 Special on Bigfoot starts, and just as they start running new footage of the beast, my wife Kelly walks in front of the television set with a pink sexy Victoria Secret "teddy" lingerie on and in sexy pose says, "Do you want to get intimate?" I yell, "Move away from the television!"

She stomps away up the stairs hurt and rejected. Don't judge me too harshly, this was before I had a DVR and could record programs, <u>this will be the only chance I get to see this documentary</u>. This is before the age of YouTube where I can look up videos I have missed.

Before I die, I want to self-righteously proclaim to my skeptic friends, "See…the Squatch is real!"

There was intimacy later that evening, but not before some yelling and tears and anger and some statement about "….maybe you should marry a Sasquatch and have sex with it," in a smart aleck-y kind-a way. Choosing between sex and new Big Foot home movie clips was an easy decision in 2006. In the age of computers and YouTube, sex ALWAYS gets priority from me.

Fire, Fire, Fire – 1990's (8)

1993 is the summer
after Seminary graduation.
I paint the home of the creator of
McGruff the Crime Dog
nest the Hudson River in Piermont NY,
with classmate Edward
before he heads to Yale.

At the end of the work day,
we drink a beer and watch
the MTV cartoon Beavis and Butthead,
two clueless and ignorant teen-agers,
pyromaniacs who say, "Fire, fire, fire!" and
and call each other "Cornholio."
It is sophomoric in humor,
and perfect for this time in my life
before entering ministry.

I live in the world of the profane and prophets,
of the sacred and the secular.
Trying to be a true follower is
confusing, exhausting, guilt-ridden
and impossible for me.
Grace, pardons, learning the lessons – repeat.
The apostle Paul had the same problem
2,000 years earlier.
Laughter is a coping mechanism
with my sea sickness on
the Earth Ship journey.

SECTION 5

QUEENS NY NEIGHBOR JIMMY (1)

It was a few days after the 9/11 attack (2001),
when I ran into my neighbors,
Jill and Jimmy at the corner bodega.
I frequently ran into them there.

Jimmy, a custodian, worked in a building
two blocks from the Towers.

He told me on top of his building
were airplane seats, airplane parts
and body parts as well.

Two weeks after the attack, I ran into Jill at the
bodega, and she looked like hell. "Hi Jill.
Where is Jimmy?"

"You haven't heard? Jimmy had
a heart attack! He's dead!"

I gave her a hug and condolences.

Imagine that, surviving a 9/11 attack
only to die 10 days later.

If I had a choice, I would choose the
terrorist attack, it gives family and friends a better
story. Victims always get more sympathy.

Juvenile Detention Student (2)

It was my first year teaching
in NYC in 1999.
In the middle of the year,
A tall African American teen
walks into my class.
He shows me his schedule
and he is in my class.

Nothing unusual, the
school is a 50-50 mix of
African American and Dominican.
When I ask where he came
From he says, "Spafford."

I later ask my union representative,
"What is Spafford?"
I am informed it is
a juvenile detentions center
in the Bronx.

The next day I ask the new
student why he was sent to Spafford
and he tells me, "In my last school,
I punched my teacher in the face."

I look at him and say,
"Welcome to my classroom."
The kid sat in the back of the class
and never gave me a problem.

BRUCE LEE ZEN MEDITATION (3)

VARSITY PRINTING TEAM (4)
1981

In 1981 at William Allen High School in the printing department, a student makes a money tree for an Uncle, and uses printing shop machines to created $5 dollar bills for the money tree.

In February of 1981, the Secret Service show up to investigate who was creating fuzzy $1 and $5 bills that were turning up at the local arcade, pizza shops and downtown 6th Street hooker circuit. It turns out a 17 year old had printed approximately $11,000 of counterfeit money. Why work for your money when you can let your counterfeited money work for you?

The news makes the Allentown Morning Call, and went national in Time Magazine and even lands as a joke on the Johnny Carson Show.

Labor is the amount of time spent making money that represents the value of goods and services. Counterfeiting is theft and undercuts the value of money. You are receiving goods and services, without having put in your time in labor for the value of the goods and services. There is a reason work is called work – it takes energy to make a living.

The following year, t-shirts are printed up at the William Allen High School saying "Varsity Printing Team," and on the backs have the image of a $5 bill. That is funny.

HE LISTENED TO ADVICE (5)

He always asked for advice and when I shard my life experience with him he said "Yea, yea, yea…I'm gonna do that!"

He was so convincing, I always thought he was going to carry through.

He listened to advice, but he never followed though, because that is what many alcoholics do.

When he asked why I know longer gave advice, I told him, "What's the point? You never follow through."

He said, "No, this time I am going to follow through! Yea, yea, yea – I really am!"

I just knew he would not follow through…and he did not. I could only pray he hit bottom and got help before killing someone on the road.

He died never reaching out help, but at least he did not kill anyone drunk driving his truck.

Love the person, hate the disease.

PARTY LIKE ITS 1999! (5)
1982

I was aged 16 when Prince's song "Party Like Its 1999," came out in 1982. In 1982 I was a high school sophomore and 1999 was 17 years away. In 1999, I would be 31 years old. That seemed like lifetimes away.

What would I be doing in 1999? I figured I would have finished college and grad school and been a pastor at a Christian and Missionary Alliance Church of 75 people somewhere in central Pennsylvania where I would go hunting and fishing. I would be married and have 2-3 kids as well.

In October of 1999 I began the career of being a high school history teacher in NYC. I had served as a minister from 1993 through 1999. I am married but have no kids. My 1982 prediction was only off by one state and three kids.

1999 comes and goes, and apparently Prince must have thought the world was going to end in the year 2,000. It did not. However, in 2016, Prince did die, and it came 17 years after 1999. Prince died at age 57 and was reported he to play 157 instruments. I can play the kazoo and the radio – making two for me.

In 2016, I am aged 51. Time flies. I am going to party like every day is my last day. I just hope I can collect Social Security for at least seven years or longer.

THE TEAMSTER (6)
June 2018

As Helen and I are checking out of the Regis Hotel in Wildwood Crest Hotel, a brute of a man is standing next to us with a blue shirt some emblem on his shirt.

He approximately 5'6, not necessarily tall, with his dark hair and brown eyes, but has the body and arms of a professional wrestler. He looks like the muscle for one of the Mafia families. I bet his name is Tony.

I look at his shirt two to three times to figure out what the emblem is and recognize it is the Teamsters Union Horse Head symbol. The union for United Parcel Service and most truck drivers. Jimmy Hoffa, one of the original organizers of the union was notorious for using muscle to intimidate bosses or to make sure the workers were given living wages, benefits and treated as humans instead of machines, for the important truckers they play in the American economy.

If only all unions had called a national strike

when President Reagan fired all the PATCO airline traffic controllers in 1981, perhaps organized labor would consist of 20-25% of workers today.

Tony the Teamster looks at me wondering why I keep looking at him.

I say, "I apologize for staring. I see your emblem is of the Teamsters. Go Teamsters!"

He smiles.

I say, "I wish our Teachers union operated like the Teamsters."

He nods and gives the knowing look.

As we drive home, I see him at the laundry truck with a clip as the laundry baskets are being taken off the truck.

Solidarity forever – for the Teamsters anyway.

How will the Teamsters respond to the self-driving trucks coming in the near future? Time will tell.

Past Presidents Advising #45 (7)

"No president who performs his duties faithfully and
conscientiously can have any leisure."
-Pres. Polk

"The test of our progress is not that we add to the
abundance of those who have much, but if we provide
enough to have too little."   **-Pres. FDR**

"The disenfranchisement of a single legal of a single legal
elector by fraud or intimidation is a crime too grave to
be regarded lightly."   **-Pres. B. Harrison**

"He who serves his party best who serves his country best."
-Pres. Hayes

"The ship of democracy, which has weathered all storms,
may sink through the mutiny of those on board."
-Pres. Cleveland

"Truth is the glue that holds our governments together.
Compromise is the oil that makes governments go."
-Pres. Ford

"The most important thing to do this job is to have big
chunks of time during the day when all you're doing is
thinking."   **-Pres. Obama**

1990's: Tata [Father] (8)

Anti-Apartheid Leader

Nelson Mandela

sent to Robin's Island Prison

27 years accused a subversive.

Mandela released

is elected President of

South Africa and transitions

the country apartheid free -

a graceful bitter-free

subversion success story.

SECTION 6

WHY DIDN'T JESUS VISIT ALLENTOWN? (1)

I am in third grade
and my Sunday School teacher is telling
a story about Jesus.

Every week I hear about places
such as
Nazareth,
Bethlehem,
Emmaus and
Egypt.

These were all towns
surrounding Allentown Pa.

"Ms. Van Skyke,
Why didn't Jesus visit Allentown?
It is much nicer than Bethlehem!"

I had to go college
in New York to learn
about history in my county
in Pennsylvania.

The biblical names were
mission outposts to reach
Native Americans
by the followers of Jon Hus,
or the Moravian Church
to fulfill the
Great Commission
of Jesus Christ.

SELLING SUBS FOR THE TEAM (2)

I stop by the Stop-n-Shop food store
to pick up some items after work.

In front of the store are
Some high school soccer players
Selling tickets for a car wash
On this hot-humid summer
August day.

I think back to my little
League football year with
the Alton Park Comets
football team,

selling brooms,
raffle tickets,
hoagies

for new night lights.

In Allentown we call them hoagies,
at the shore they call them subs,
and in New England they call
the sandwiches grinders.

I hated going door to door
selling "stuff," but it
was part of being on a team.

In the Stop-n-Shop, I buy
a pack of Double Chocolate
ice cream bars,
three for $4.50.

As I exit the store,
I drop a dollar in the
Donation bucket and hand
Ice cream bars to the two
high school kids.

Their eyes light up.

I say, "I hope my contribution
helps make your fundraising
efforts a little sweeter."

One smiles,
the other
nods in
appreciation.

Harlot Story #3   (3)
(Summer 1994)

I was working as a pastor at New
Life Fellowship in Elmhurst Queens.
Elmhurst is the most ethnically diverse
area of the United States.

My apartment was on the border of
Long Island City and Astoria,
one block away from the Steinway
Street Subway Stop and two blocks
away from the Kaufman Astoria Studios
where they filmed Sesame Street and
The Cosby Show.

I use to drive to Astoria Park with
the famous Hell Gates Bridge made
famous in "The French Connection,"
and with an astounding view of the
Triborough Bridge and Manhattan skyline.

One morning as I was sitting in my car
at 34th Avenue and 43rd Street, where there
was a white trash bar on that street, stood
an Asian woman at 7:30 am in the morning.

She walks over to the passenger open window
and says, "Where are you going?"

I am going to Astoria Park for a jog.
"May I get a ride with you? I live near there."
Sure. Hop on in.

She says, "I really appreciate this. I would be willing to do anything to show my appreciation."

No, no, no. I am happy to give you a ride to Astoria. "They say eating is not cheating!"

Okay Miss - LISTEN - 1) I am married and 2) I am a pastor and I am just taking you to Astoria Park.

She crosses her arms and is upset with me. As we get closer to the Park she says, "Make a left here!"

Listen Miss, I am going Astoria Park, I am not a taxi service. I do not like her attitude and I pull over.

"What are you doing?"
I am pulling over. You are going to get out of the car, and say thank you for me driving you into Astoria.

She gets out of the car, slams the door and yells "F__ you" at me.

I attend the weekly Church Staff meeting and tell them what happened. One of the co-pastors says, "You are lucky she did not scratch your face and start yelling rape! Your picture would have been on the cover of all the NYC dailies saying "Pastor Attempts Rape!"

I am grateful I am not in prison with an attorney trying to explain to the wife and church elders what really happened. I learn an important ministry and life lesson.

WASHING MY SHOES (4)
Spring of 1973

I am aged 8 in third grade with Ms. Ott. She has blond hair, eye glasses, and sometimes moody. On this Spring day at 3pm, my 3 mile walk home in dress shoes begins.

Next to Union Terrace Elementary is the Union Terrace Pond. I walk along the pond with my hard plastic bottomed dress shoes, and slip on the mud and take end up in the pond. I land on my feet, and I am in one foot of water. It is as if the pond contains a large magnet in the lake, and my shoes were made out of nickel, iron and cobolt and pulled me right in.

As I am walking along the edge of the pond, a yellow pick-up truck with the Allentown Pennsylvania insignia pulls along the sidewalk, and I look to see it is my Uncle Fritz who is driving it. Uncle Fritz is a city worker and the family clown, and for sure, this story is going to be shared with my eight pairs of Aunts and Uncles and dozens of cousins at Nana Geist's house this coming Sunday.

"Jimmy, what are you doing? Why are you in the Union
    Terrace Pond in your dress clothes?"
I answer, *"What do you think? I am washing my be-damn*
    shoes!"

THIS story I must endure for the rest of my life at every Geist Christmas Family Party and Uncle Fritz laughs and wheezes every time. When I think back, such a witty and snarky answer for an eight year old to give his smart alek Uncle.

88

FISH WALK (5)
1995

Uncle Tom and Aunt Adele bought a lovely home near
Mount Pocono that had a pond on it and was surrounded by
Pennsylvania State Game Lands.

I lived in New York City at the time and any chance I got
to go hunting up there was an opportunity to commune with
nature and enjoy my Aunt and Uncle's company. Uncle
Tom is a funny guy, good union man and has a heart for the
poor and oppressed as Jesus does, except Uncle Tom
curses more than the Son of Mankind.

On one summer trip to their Pocono retreat home, Uncle
Tom said, "I like to take my fish for a walk." In his pond
were all types of trout. The pond once attracted and otter,
and a blue crane, that killed many trout.

I thought to myself, *How do you take a fish for a walk?*
Uncle Tom was known for telling tall tales sometimes. Do
you put a collar and leash on the fish and drag it for 15-20
feet before throwing it back in the pond?

We went for a nature hike, and as we passed the pond,
sure enough, you could see the fish following Uncle Tom
as he walked by, especially the palomino fish. He really
did take his fish for a walk.

When you feed the fish, they follow you hoping for the
next hand out.

BANANAS AND PEACHES (6)
1978

It is Thanksgiving time, and my family, Uncle Bob's family, Nana Ruby, Uncle Bill and Aunt Corrine and Nana and Grandpa at sitting at the table with myself, sister Jody and cousins Chrissy, Jason and Becky. Four year old Becky says in the middle of the meal, "Boys have bananas and girls have peaches." The adults laugh and say, "That is true."

In April 2018 I am teaching a 7th grade class in at P.S. 24 in Paterson New Jersey, when a student yells, "Look at the board!" Someone has drawn a picture of the male sexual organ on the black board and the class goes into a tizzy.

I say, "Class, calm down, that is called a penis. You should have learned about this in health class." It was a way of calming down the hysteria before fainting and foaming mouths took over The following day I am summoned into the Principal's office with my supervisor.

"Mr. Geist, is it true you said 'penis' in your classroom?"
"Yes," and explain what happened and why I said it.
I am told, don't use that word in front of your 7th graders.

I am surprised "my 7th graders", quite adept to cursing like sailors and dropping "f-bombs" in class, could be so shocked by a word found in the school biology book and Webster dictionary. Penis is a dirty word at PS24.

Perhaps if I had called the drawing a "dick," the children would have been less offended and not snitched on teacher.

My friend Terry has been hounding me to visit him in Florida to go fishing with his buddies. I finally take the plunge and fly to visit him in the fishing capital of the world. I envision heat, humidity, mosquitoes and possible alcohol poisoning.

Terry's shiny state of the art fishing boat comes out of a Bass Fishing Catalog. We fish the lake behind his house and I have fun on his boat with three other decent salt of the earth red-necks.

The trip was mostly successful, we did catch fish. Terry's friend took a break and sat on the edge of the boat with his feet dangling in the water when he screamed and pulled up his foot with two missing toes and blood flowing into the water of the boat floor boards.

He was bit by what is called a Pacu, a fish related to the Piranha, that can get up to 50 pounds and have teeth the size of human teeth, but razor sharp like sharks teeth, or a vampires teeth.

We are under a tree at the time, when a branch falls out of the tree, but it turns out to be a water moccasin snake, and in panic of five grown men jumping around the boat, Terrys friend #2 is bitten in the leg. Terry's friend number three faints while looking at the snake, missing toes and blood in the boat and falls into the lake. Before we can pull him into the boat, a giant Florida Gator grabs him by the arm.

Terry and I are the only two who have not been attacked by Florida's wildlife, and we grab friend #3's legs. The gator goes into a death spin, and friend #3's arm gets ripped off. We are now able to pull him into the boat.

Terry says, "We need to get back to my dock to get help from the paramedics!" As he is driving his boat at full throttle back home, a black widow spider lowers itself from the steering wheel consul and bites Terry on the thigh.

Terry is able to steer us back to the dock, and I run in front of the house to flag down the ambulances. The E.M.T.'s walk around the house to the four wounded guys laying on shore, one with missing toes, one with a snake bite, one with a missing arm and Terry, who now is in a 15 foot Burmese python constriction wrapping.

As they say, "A bad day of fishing, is better than a good day at work."

VELOCIPEDE SHOPPING via 1956 (7)

My father Bill and his buddy Joe
use to hang together as kids.
They use to go fishing together.
hang at the Boys Club or
shoot birds in the woods and rats
at the dump with their BB guns.
They also loved bicycles.
Popular bikes of the mid-1950's
were Western Flyers, Raleighs
and the Schwinn bike models.

When you grow up poor, the way to
get a bicycle was to go to the police
 station storage to see which abandoned
bikes had been picked up by the police.
If no one claimed the two-wheeler
within 30 days, a young person could
claim the lost mode of transportation
on the 31st day of the discarding.

Bill and Joe went to the station to check
out the velocipedes that they liked best,
and showed up on the 31st day to
claim their anticipated peddled freedom.
The buddies prayed and dreamt hoping
their prizes would not be claimed nor
swiped by some other poor kid before they
got to the Allentown Police Storage Unit;
the greatest day ever, or of disappointment.
They just picked out another until victory.

93

CLASSROOM ENFORCER (8)

(circa 2008)

There are times I get excited about teaching a lesson.
I have taken time to research and put a lesson together,
and look forward to imparting the knowledge to the
youngsters. It will be one of my greatest lessons!

In the back of the Washington Heights NYC class
room is a student who was always in trouble, always
in the Principal's Office, and always getting
suspensions. A meeting is called with the parents and
it is made clear, Malik must change his ways, or it is
time for him to be expelled. This semester, Malik
becomes more respectful and begins doing his work.
He wants to get his diploma and walk in graduation.

 In the second row is Jose and Raymond. They are not
paying attention to the lesson I have bled for. They are
talking and laughing and making it hard for the serious
students to hear what I am saying. My frustration level
is about to hit boiling point when "the Enforcer"
speaks. Malik says, "SHUT THE F**K UP! I AM
TRYING TO LEARN HERE, AND YOU
KNUCKLE-HEADS ARE BEING
DISRESPECTFUL!"

You can hear a pin drop - and Raymond and Jose
make the "OMG face," and don't say another word the
rest of the period, because Malik is angry, bigger than
them, and <u>will</u> kick their arses after school.

I wish I had an enforcer in every class I taught.

OPPOSITIONAL DEFIANT DISORDER (8)
December 2018

Highlander Refocusing Center or the In-House
Suspension of the local high school rules:
    Students must sign in.
    No talking.
    No cell phones.
    Computers only for school work – no videos.
    Lunch to be brought to the H.R.C. room.
    No French fries.

The student says, "I want a chicken sandwich with
    mayo, French fries, orange vitamin water and hot
    ranch sauce."
Sorry, no fries.
Why not?
HRC rule.
Who made that rule up?
I don't know.
I want to talk with the A.P.
Why?
This is the most stupid rule ever.
Is it?
I want to talk with the A.P.
Fine.

I think, "This would never happen in the Turkish
Prison I saw in the movie 'Midnight Express.'"

Books of Poetry & Anecdotes by
James Curtis Geist
*Selected Poems for Volume II

Bottom of the Food Chain (2017)

Horse Shoe for Good Luck   The King & the Dog
Sales Pitch   Dental Partials
Vagal Reflex   Queens Neighbor Jimmy
Elks Lodge Beauty Contest   Nemesis
Why Didn't Jesus Visit Allentown?

Poetry for the Kathy Lee Gifford Child Labor
Sweatshop Retirement Village (2017)

The Finicky Beggar   Good Bye Dream
Death by Painting   Juvenile Detention Student
Garden Faucet   Selling Subs for the Team
Harlem Mocking Bird Attack

A Robot Ate My Homework (2018)

Sic!   Hooker Story #2
Yes Sir Madame Teacher   Hooker Story #3
Gift from the Forest God   Bruce Lee Zen Meditation
Drill Sergeant

Time Rich & Cash Poor (2018)

Queens Laundromat Robbery   The Call
Last Church Play   Varsity Printing Team
The Wind Cries Mary   Washing My Shoes
Turkey, Bear or Bobcat?

Books of Poetry & Anecdotes by
James Curtis Geist
*Selected Poems for Volume II

Wonder Years of Teenaged Insecurity (2018)

Elementary School Porn

Do You Model?

Broken Down Freightliner

Fish Walk

Wipe Out

Party Like it is 1999

He Listened to Advice

Guns & Butter; Bread & Roses (2018)

Happiness When…

Early Schedule

Future Teachers of America

Fishing Capital of the World

The Teamster

Bananas & Peaches

Napper or Corpse?

Stories of the Heilige, Polter & Zeitgeist (2019)

My Child Polter

Gringo Halloween

Chainsaw Love

The Price of Truth Telling

Mammogram Phone Call

Velocipede Shopping 1956

Advice for #45

Ragbag (2019)

Erin Go Braugh

Forty-Eight

10th Grade Spanish Class

Oppositional Defiant Disorder

Nelson Mandela

Classroom Enforcer

Fire, Fire, Fire